POWIS
CASTLE

Powys

THE NATIONAL TRUST

Acknowledgements

This new guidebook draws heavily on that written by Christopher Rowell in 1986 and on the picture entries in that guide by Alastair Laing. The Trust is grateful to the Earl of Powis and the Powis Estate Trustees for permission to examine the family papers and to reproduce the Oliver miniature of Lord Herbert of Chirbury and the 1771 Pritchard survey. George Herbert generously shared his profound knowledge of the history and genealogy of his family. The descriptions of the Antique sculpture, textiles and clocks are based on notes compiled by Dr Susan Walker, George Wingfield-Digby and Jonathan Betts. The Trust is also grateful to Frances Buckland, John Cornforth, Anthony du Boulay, Joe Earle, Jonathan Harris and Robert Skelton for their help. Thanks to the generous and continuing support of the National Heritage Memorial Fund and the National Art Collections Fund, several major works of art remain in the castle.

Photographs: Photographic Survey, Courtauld Institute of Art pp. 44, 51 (top); National Library of Wales p. 36; National Trust pp. 45 (bottom), 51 (bottom), back cover; National Trust Photographic Library pp. 33, 39, 50 (bottom left); NTPL/John Bethell p. 46 (top right); NTPL/Andrew Butler pp. 4, 5, 37 (top), 38 (top and bottom), 41, 46 (bottom left); NTPL/Andreas von Einsiedel front cover, pp. 7, 9, 10 (top), 11, 14 (bottom), 16, 17, 19, 20, 26, 27, 28, 31, 32 (bottom left), 47; NTPL/Christopher Gallagher p. 26; NTPL/John Hammond pp. 8, 10 (bottom), 12, 13, 14 (top), 15, 18, 21, 22, 23, 25, 30, 32 (top left), 42 (top and bottom), 43 (top and bottom), 45 (top left and right), 48 (top), 49, 50 (top), 52 (top and bottom); NTPL/Erik Pelham pp. 1, 32 (bottom right); NTPL/Ian Shaw p. 37 (bottom); NTPL/J. Whitaker p. 29.

Designed and typeset by James Shurmer (31.5.06)
Printed by Hawthornes for National Trust (Enterprises) Ltd, Heelis, Kemble Drive, Swindon, Wilts SN2 2NA

(*Front cover*) The State Bedroom
(*Title-page*) Tiger-head finial from Tipu Sultan's throne, 1787–93 (Clive Museum)
(*Back cover*) Chintz hanging from Tipu Sultan's tent, c.1725–50 (Clive Museum). Acquired with the help of the National Art Collections Fund

Bibliography

Most of the Powis Castle papers are deposited in the National Library of Wales, Aberystwyth, in the India Office Library, London, and in the Shropshire Record Office, Shrewsbury.

Anon., 'Herbertiana', *Montgomeryshire Collections*, v, London, 1872, pp. 153–98, 353–94; viii, 1875, pp. 1–46; Anon., 'Powis Castle', *Country Life*, 9 May 1908, pp. 666–72; Anon., 'The Biggest Oaks in Britain: Famous Trees at Powis Castle', *Country Life*, 22 June 1935, pp. 647–9; Bingley, Rev. W., *A Tour round North Wales performed during the Summer of 1798*, third edition, 1838, ii, pp. 4–11; Bridgeman, Hon. and Rev. G.T.O., 'The Princes of Upper Powys', *Collectanea Archaeologica*, 1862, reprinted in *Montgomeryshire Collections*; Byng, Hon. John [Viscount Torrington], *The Torrington Diaries*, ed. by C. Bruyn Andrews, London, 1936, i, pp. 137–8 [1784]; iii, pp. 294–6 [1793]; Cornforth, John, 'Powis Castle, Powys', *Country Life*, 9 July 1987, pp. 106–11; Croft-Murray, Edward, *Decorative Painting in England 1537–1837*, London, 1962; Davies, R.R., *Conquest, Coexistence, and Change in Wales 1063–1415*, Oxford, 1987; *Dictionary of Welsh Biography*, Honourable Society of Cymmrodorion, 1959; Dineley, Thomas, *The Account of the Official Progress of His Grace Henry the 1st Duke of Beaufort through Wales in 1684*, facsimile edition, London, 1888, pp. 67–9, 73, 156 [MS in British Library]; Evans, Rev. J., *The Beauties of England and Wales*, 1809, xxiv, pp. 876–85; Girouard, Mark, 'A Welsh Fortress veiled in Antiquity: Powis Castle, Montgomeryshire', *Country Life Annual*, 1967; Hadfield, Miles, 'Who was the Maker of Powis Gardens?', *Gardeners Chronicle*, 20 April 1966, pp. 401–2; Hall, Michael, 'Powis Castle, Powys', *Country Life*, 21 October 1993, pp. 80–3; Hussey, Christopher, 'Powis Castle', *Country Life*, 30 May, 6, 13 and 20 June 1936, pp. 564–72, 598–604, 624–30, 652–8; Ionides, Julia, *Thomas Farnolls Pritchard of Shrewsbury*, 1999, pp. 186–94; Jones, Morris Charles, *The Feudal Barons of Powys*, London, 1868, reprinted in *Montgomeryshire Collections*; Laing, Alastair, 'Lord Herbert of Cherbury', *National Art Collections Fund Annual Review*, 1991, pp. 147–52; Lawson, James, and Merlin Waterson, 'Pritchard as Architect and Antiquary at Powis', *National Trust Yearbook 1975–6*, 1976, pp. 8–11; Lewis, W.J., *Lead Mining in Wales*, University of Wales Press, Cardiff, 1967, pp. 147–59; Loveday, John, *Diary of a Tour in the Year 1732*, Roxburghe Club, 1890; Lyttelton, George, Lord, 1756, printed in *A Gentleman's Tour through Monmouthshire and Wales in the months of June and July 1774*, 1781; Murphy, Martin, 'Maria's Dreams: Lady Mary Herbert, 1685–1775', *Montgomeryshire Collections*, lxxxv, 1997, pp. 87–100; 'The Reckoning', lxxxvi, 1998, pp. 65–80; Parry, Edward, *Cambrian Mirror*, 1846, pp. 287–90; Pennant, Thomas, *Tours in Wales*, 1778, reprinted 1810, iii, pp. 209–15; Sinclair, Catherine, *Hill and Valley or Wales and the Welsh*, c.1833, pp. 93–7; Smith, W. J., ed., *Herbert Correspondence*, University of Wales Press, Cardiff, 1968, pp. 17–45; Spiker, Dr S. H., *Travels through England*, 1816, translated 1820; Tipping, H. Avray, 'Powis Castle', *Country Life*, 3 and 10 February 1917, pp. 108–15, 132–9.

CONTENTS

POWIS CASTLE

Fortress and Family Home

High on its narrow ridge, Powis Castle commands panoramic views over the Severn Valley towards England. On the terraces below lies Powis's world-famous garden. Inspired by the formal gardens of France and Italy, it combines 18th-century lead statues with intensely colourful planting. Within the red castle walls is a family home that has been remodelled and embellished over more than 400 years to reflect the changing needs and ambitions of the Herbert family, who keep an apartment here.

The Powis terraces spread over five levels. The long history of Powis can also be divided into five stages:

- The castle began life as the medieval fortress of the Welsh princes of Powys, who held on to their kingdom despite the threats from their more powerful neighbours in Gwynedd and England.

- In 1587 Powis was sold to an English nobleman, Sir Edward Herbert, who created the romantic Long Gallery, which is richly decorated with the coats of arms of his ancestors.

- From the 1660s, the 1st Marquess of Powis remodelled the interior on a palatial scale, creating the Grand Staircase and the magnificent suite of baroque rooms on the first floor, including the State Bedroom. He also laid out the garden terraces, but was forced into exile in 1688 because of his loyalty to the deposed King James II.

- In 1784 the marriage of Lady Henrietta Herbert and Edward Clive united the Powis and Clive estates. Edward was the son of Robert Clive, the conqueror of India, and he enriched the superb collection of treasures from the Indian subcontinent which is now displayed in the Clive Museum.

- In the early 20th century the 4th Earl of Powis redecorated much of the castle in Jacobean style, while his wife Violet brought the garden back to life, introducing new varieties from all over the world, which form the basis for the present planting.

At Powis, each generation has added something new, softening, without obliterating, the achievements of the past. Symbolising this gradual evolution are the clipped yews of the 1st Marquess's garden, which with the years have grown and melted over the terrace walls so that now they perfectly complement the austere architecture of the castle above.

(Left) The view from the terraces at dawn
(Right) The Powis terraces

TOUR OF THE CASTLE

THE GRAND STAIRCASE

William, 1st Marquess of Powis would have led honoured guests in formal procession up these splendidly decorated stairs to his State Apartments on the floor above. The staircase was probably constructed for Lord Powis by William Winde between 1674, when he bought an earldom, and 1687, when he was created a marquess (an earl's coronet appears above the Powis coat of arms on the painted ceiling).

CEILING AND WALL-PAINTINGS

Gerard Lanscroon painted the walls of the Lower Hall in 1705 with convincingly three-dimensional statues in niches and huge vases of flowers over the doors — a foretaste of the illusionistic skills he showed in depicting the gods and goddesses on the main stairs. The *Drunken Silenus led by Satyrs* on the lower ceiling is loosely derived from an engraving by Andrea Mantegna (1431–1506).

You can see the paintings on the stairs more easily from the upper landing, and so they are described on p. 24.

SCULPTURE

On the chest at the foot of the stairs is a bust of Spencer Perceval, Prime Minister from 1809 until 1812, when he was assassinated by a madman in the House of Commons. The other bust is of Charles, 1st Lord Farnborough (1761–1838), who left part of his picture collection to the National Gallery.

THE PRIVATE DINING ROOM

The 6th Earl of Powis used this as a family dining room until his death in 1988. Before that, it was the Smoking Room, where gentlemen retired after dinner in the Dining Room.

PICTURES

In the window recess opposite the door is an 18th-century Dutch townscape. The overmantel of *Two Cupids flanking a Vase* built into the panelling is 17th-century.

FURNITURE

Surrounding the 18th-century mahogany dining-table is a 'harlequin' set of Georgian dining-chairs of five patterns.

The walnut-veneered longcase clock, c.1680, wound only once a month, is by Thomas Tompion, the father of British clockmaking.

The tables either side of the clock are Milanese, late 18th-century, with later tops.

The pair of ormolu (gilt bronze) candelabra, c.1810, is signed by Thomire of Paris.

The French ormolu centrepiece, c.1830, is known as a *surtout de table.* The mirrored top was designed to reflect ornaments placed on it.

The ormolu chandelier is English, c.1820.

TEXTILES

The large Brussels tapestry, c.1580, depicts Esau being reconciled with his twin brother Jacob, who had bought his inheritance for a 'mess of pottage'. The machine-made carpet has a Khotan (eastern Turkestan) design.

CERAMICS

The Chinese blue-and-white porcelain of the Kangxi and Qianlong periods (1662–1795) was collected by the 6th Lord Powis when a student in the 1920s.

(Right) The lower landing of the Grand Staircase

The Dining Room in 1905; watercolour by H. C. Brewer

THE DINING ROOM

This is the first room you see of those transformed in 1902–4 for George, 4th Earl of Powis. He commissioned the architect G. F. Bodley to dismantle a bedroom and adjoining pantry to create a new formal dining room in a richly decorated Jacobean style, which he thought more in keeping with the ancient castle. It was also conveniently placed for the Kitchen, reached by the back stairs on the left.

EARLIER HISTORY

This was possibly the site of the medieval Great Hall, and by 1684 it was already being used as a dining room. By 1772 it had been divided to form, at the near end, a panelled Common Parlour, where those on business waited to see Lord Powis in his nearby study. During the first half of the 19th century it again served as a dining room, which was described as 'dark and gloomy'; later, it became the 'Staircase Bedroom'.

CHIMNEYPIECES

Lord Powis asked Bodley to design new oak chimneypieces based on ones he greatly admired in a Jacobean room from Bromley-by-Bow Palace in London, which the Victoria & Albert Museum had rescued after the building was demolished in 1893. They are decorated with the arms of Lord Powis (on the left) and his Countess, the 16th Baroness Darcy de Knayth (on the right). Her full-length portrait hangs on the opposite wall.

PLASTERWORK AND PANELLING

Fragments of 16th-century plasterwork survive in the window alcove and above the exit door. Bodley based his new plasterwork on the ceiling of the old

Reindeer Inn at Banbury. The style of the panelling was derived from the Jacobean woodwork of the old pantry.

PICTURES

1 *Hon. Rebecca Clive, Mrs Robinson* (1760–95) by GEORGE ROMNEY
The eldest daughter of Clive of India.

2 *Lady Henrietta Herbert, Countess of Powis* (1758–1830) by Sir JOSHUA REYNOLDS
The last of the original Herberts of Powis. By her marriage to Edward, 2nd Lord Clive, their estates passed to the Clive family.

3 *Hon. Charlotte Clive* (1762–95) by GEORGE ROMNEY, 1783–5
Rebecca Clive's younger sister, she also died young.

11 *Lady Eleanor Percy, Lady Powis* (1582/3–1650), ENGLISH, 1595
The wife of William, 1st Lord Powis (no.12). Her Book of Hours and rosary are displayed in the Gateway Room (see p. 15).

12 *William Herbert, 1st Lord Powis* (1574–1656), ENGLISH, 1595
During the Civil War he held Powis for the King until it was captured in 1644.

14 *Violet Lane-Fox, Countess of Powis* (1865–1929) by ELLIS ROBERTS
She brought the garden back to life in 1911 (see p. 35). Wife of 4th Earl (no. 17).

17 *George Herbert, 4th Earl of Powis* (1862–1952) by Sir WILLIAM LLEWELLYN
The creator of this room, and the donor of Powis to the National Trust in 1952.

65 *Lady Mary Herbert, Viscountess Montagu* (1659–1744/5) by FRANÇOIS DE TROY
Painted around 1689 96, when she was in exile in France with her father, the 1st Marquess of Powis.

FURNITURE

The mahogany dining-chairs are c.1755 in the style of Thomas Chippendale (1718–79) and retain their original needlework upholstery.

*The English mahogany dining-table, c.*1725, had Coromandel banding added in the Regency period.

The three oak tables are English, mid-17th-century.

The horseshoe-shaped table in front of the second fireplace is a wine table supplied by Burrey & White of Shrewsbury c.1810. At this period, male diners would often retire to the fireside for a protracted drinking session with their cronies at a table like this. The Powis example has a curtain as a protector against the heat and a net for the empty bottles. The two coasters held the bottles: unless they were secured in this way, the narrow surface of the horse-shoe top increased the likelihood of accidents.

TEXTILES AND CERAMICS

The carpets were presumably made for the room after Bodley's alterations. *The china* includes Japanese Imari vases and a Chinese *wucai* vase, *c.*1660.

Outside the Dining Room door is the hot plate: the Kitchen was at the foot of the service stairs. *Ascend the stairs to the Library on the first floor.* The tunnel-vaulted ceiling of the Library vestibule was painted by Lanscroon, with a seated depiction of Pax (Peace) being brought olive fronds and laurel crowns by cupids.

The horseshoe-shaped wine table was designed for comfortable fireside drinking

The State Apartments

Around the Long Gallery on the first floor of the medieval castle, William, 1st Marquess of Powis created a suite of grand rooms in the 1660s in which to receive distinguished visitors. Much of his work still survives.

THE LIBRARY

This was fitted up *c.*1665 as an ante-room 'hung with old tapestry' between the two State Rooms now called the Blue and Oak Drawing Rooms. The blue and gold wooden cornice survives from this period.

In 1841–2 Lord Powis added the bookcases and he probably had the red and gold embossed wall-paper put up at the same time.

CEILING PAINTING

Gerard Lanscroon decorated the ceiling about 1705 with an allegorical composition incorporating portraits of the 2nd Marquess's daughters: seated in the clouds are Lady Mary Herbert as Minerva, Goddess of Wisdom, and Theresa, Lady Throckmorton as

(Above) The Library

Lord Herbert of Chirbury as a melancholy knight; miniature by Isaac Oliver

Truth; two younger sisters lean over the balustrade. Lady Mary was badly miscast, as she almost ruined the family with her unwise financial speculating (see p. 42).

(see p. 42)

WINDOW

The high window overlooks the great stone stairway leading up to the east tower – the main entrance to the castle until the late 18th century. The park is screened off by the Marquess Gates, so-called because they were made, probably in 1707, for the 2nd Marquess, whose daughters appear in the Library ceiling.

SCULPTURE

The bust of Edward Herbert, 1st Baron Herbert of Chirbury (1581/3–1648), dated 1631, is by Hubert Le Sueur (c.1585–c.1660). Lord Herbert was a poet, philosopher and diplomat. He wrote what is perhaps the first secular autobiography in English and was probably the most portrayed man of his day outside royalty. His great-great-grandson inherited Powis in 1748. Herbert may have met Le Sueur at the court of Louis XIII, where he was British ambassador in 1619–24. In 1625 Le Sueur introduced the art of bronze sculpture to Britain.

Lord Herbert of Chirbury; bronze bust by Hubert Le Sueur, 1631

The bust was sold by the family in 1962, but was bought jointly in 1990 by the National Museum of Wales and the National Trust, with the aid of the National Heritage Memorial Fund and the National Art Collections Fund.

BOOKS

In 1816, according to the Rev. Dr Spiker: 'The new library, a small modern room from which there is a fine view of the garden, we found to be entirely filled with French books which had been purchased by the young Lord Clive, then just returned from France.'

PICTURES

18 *The Madonna and Child with SS Louis of Toulouse and ?Catherine of Genoa* by ANTONIO VASILACCHI (L'ALIENSE)
Painted by a follower of the 16th-century Venetian artist Tintoretto. St Catherine's love of God and her fellow men is symbolised by the flaming heart in her breast. Bought by Clive of India in 1771.

21 *Edward Herbert, 1st Lord Herbert of Chirbury* (1581/3–1648) by ISAAC OLIVER
One of the most beautiful of all British miniatures. He is depicted here as a melancholy knight and lover.

FURNITURE

The rosewood table inlaid with brass is English, c.1810.

The settee and three chairs are English in the style of Charles II, c.1885.

The showcase to the left of the fireplace contains an 18th-century Greek cross of intricately carved boxwood (above) and a gold pectoral cross presented to Bishop Herbert (1885–1968), when Bishop of Kingston (below).

POTTERY AND PORCELAIN

The Greek and Etruscan pottery (on top of the bookcases) was made in the 4th century BC, and may have been acquired by Clive of India; his son, the 2nd Lord Clive; or George, 2nd Earl of Powis. They were all in Italy in the 1770s and 1780s. Sir William Hamilton, the British envoy in Naples and a great collector of Antique pottery, gave a small Etruscan vase to Henrietta, wife of the 2nd Lord Clive, 1st Earl of Powis.

THE OAK DRAWING ROOM

This has always been the main drawing room, to which the company would retire on great occasions, having dined in the Great Chamber (now the Blue Drawing Room).

The present decoration dates from 1902–4, when G. F. Bodley remodelled the room for the 4th Earl of Powis – the completion date appears in the frieze above the small window looking into the Inner Court. Bodley's contractors, Messrs Franklin of Deddington near Oxford, replaced a 19th-century bow-fronted sash-window with old-fashioned stone mullions, and put up the neo-Jacobean chimneypiece, plaster ceiling and frieze and the oak linenfold panelling.

Bodley took the design of his new ceiling, with its forest of pendants, from the Long Gallery at Aston Hall, Birmingham (built in 1618–35). The armorial frieze was inspired by the 16th-century plaster frieze in the Powis Long Gallery, from which casts were taken. The arms are those of the successive Herbert owners of Powis.

EARLIER HISTORY

In the window embrasure are plaster fragments, which are the sole survivors of Sir Edward Herbert's ornate decorative scheme of *c.*1593. Thomas Dineley described the room in 1684:

The fairest Roome above staires is boarded in panes and inlayd with different woods representing a stone or marble pavement, it is roof'd with a sort of fretwork ceileing shewing the Globe Celestiall all the signes of the Zodiack in figures ye Planets etc, it hath a large Chimney piece of the old fashion supporting on two Columns the Figures in bustys of SENECA and ARISTOTLE.

Above hangings of 'rich ancient Tapistrey' were 'good paintings … as big as the life' representing

The Oak Drawing Room in 1905; watercolour by H. C. Brewer

View of Verona; by Bernardo Bellotto, c.1745–7. It shows the River Adige, with the Castel San Pietro in the middle distance. Anchored in the river are wooden watermills. Bought for Powis in 1981 with the aid of the National Heritage Memorial Fund, National Art Collections Fund, Victoria & Albert Museum Grant-in-Aid scheme and private contributions

scenes from mythology. Herbert's scheme probably survived until the late 18th century, when the ceiling was replaced with another which maintained the Zodiac theme, but was in the Adam style.

PICTURES

26 *Edward Herbert, 1st Lord Herbert of Chirbury* (1581/3–1648), ENGLISH, *c.*1604
Painted in the crimson taffeta robes in which he was created a Knight of the Bath in 1604 (see no. 21, p. 11).

30 *Edward Clive, 1st Earl of Powis as a Boy* (1754–1839) by THOMAS GAINSBOROUGH, *c.*1763
About 20 years after this portrait was painted, he married Lady Henrietta Herbert and so brought the Powis estates into the Clive family. He served as Governor of Madras in 1798–1804, enriching Powis with his share of the booty captured from Tipu Sultan's palace at Seringapatam.

31 *Roger Palmer, 1st Earl of Castlemaine* (1634–1705) *and his Secretary*, attributed to SEBASTIANO BOMBELLI, 1664
Castlemaine was married to Charles II's mistress, Barbara, Duchess of Cleveland. The letter on the table is addressed to his cousin, the 1st Marquess of Powis.

33 *Robert Clive, 1st Lord Clive* (1725–74) by NATHANIEL DANCE, *c.*1770
The finest portrait of the founder of British rule in India. His son married Henrietta Herbert.

FURNITURE

The mahogany seat furniture with gilt enrichments is English, *c.*1760, and is upholstered with a green cut-silk velvet matching the curtains. The large-scale 'Pear' pattern was designed by Bodley in 1874 and supplied by Watts & Co. The cushions on the sofas are covered with a rare 18th-century Chinese silk velvet which may derive from Clive of India's collection of oriental textiles.

The day bed with green velvet cushions is English of the Charles II period, *c.*1665.

The inlaid walnut cabinets and tables, veneered with marquetry in various woods, are English, *c.*1680–90. The cabinet to the right of the alcove is later and was made to match the green-stained ivory table. Such sets are extremely rare.

The longcase clock, decorated with vases of flowers in marquetry, is English, *c.*1690. The movement is by Edward Bridgeman of Covent Garden.

The mahogany marble-topped table with central support is Italian, in the 'Napoleonic' style, *c.*1810. It may be one of the marble tables bought at the Attingham Park sale of 1828.

The white and gilt gesso fire-screen is English, *c.*1840. It contains a variety of exotic stuffed birds from Central and South America.

CERAMICS

The Greek and Etruscan pottery on the mantelpiece was made in the 4th century BC.

THE GATEWAY ROOM

This room is so called because it lies above the eastern gateway entrance to the castle. The 2nd Earl's wife, Lucy (1793–1875), and the 4th Earl's wife, Violet (1865–1929), both used it as a private sitting room. It later became a bedroom and is now used to display family relics.

EARLIER HISTORY

The room may have begun life as the dressing room to the State Bedroom across the Long Gallery (an arrangement also found at Knole in the late 17th century), although the door into the Long Gallery was not put in until about 1904 by Bodley, who also added the panelling.

FURNITURE

The cabinet nearest the fireplace is English, *c.*1690, and is decorated with laburnum wood cut in oyster shapes and arranged in radiating patterns. It was restored in the 19th century.

The cabinet by the door into the Long Gallery is also English, *c.*1670, and is similarly decorated with oyster olive veneer.

(Above)
St George and the Dragon, from Lady Powis's 15th-century Book of Hours

The 'oyster'-veneered olive wood cabinet, c.1670

The brass candlestick (converted into a lamp) is English, c.1700, and may have been made for the family chapel, which is thought to have occupied the room above. The family's Catholic faith (then illegal) may explain why the chapel was hidden away at the top of the east tower.

TAPESTRIES

The tapestries representing the Story of Nebuchadnezzar are from a set of four (the other two are in the Long Gallery). They were probably woven in the second half of the 17th century at the Great Wardrobe in Hatton Garden, London. They depict *The Triumph of Nebuchadnezzar after the Capture of Jerusalem* (nearest the fireplace) and *Daniel expounding Nebuchadnezzar's Dream*, in which a statue of gold, silver, bronze and iron, but with feet of clay, appears, symbolising the fragility of Nebuchadnezzar's mighty empire

BOOKS

The Hours of Lady Eleanor Percy, Lady Powis
The showcase to the left of the fireplace contains a 15th-century Book of Hours, which belonged to Lady Eleanor Percy (1582/3–1650), daughter of the 8th Earl of Northumberland and wife of William, 1st Lord Powis. It was produced by a commercial publishing house in the Low Countries, the source of the majority of English prayer-books of the period. The choice of subjects from the Passion rather than the Childhood of Christ, to introduce the seven times at which the faithful prayed during the day, is common in Books of Hours intended for the English market.

Mary, Queen of Scots's rosary
A Catholic like her husband, Lady Eleanor also owned the wooden rosary (shown in the 17th-century marquetry box on the centre table), which is said to have belonged to Mary, Queen of Scots.

PICTURES

38 ? *Elizabeth Spencer, Lady Craven* (1618–72), attributed to JOHN WEESOP (active 1641–?52)
Her dress is embroidered with pineapple trees, pomegranates, birds, butterflies and flowers.

40 *General Sir Percy Herbert* (1822–76)
by Sir FRANCIS GRANT
The father of the 4th Earl of Powis, he had a distinguished military career, being wounded twice during the Crimean War of 1853–6.

Cross the Long Gallery and enter the State Bedroom.

Powis from the east, on a ceramic tray in the Gateway Room

THE STATE BEDROOM

The 1st Marquess of Powis's State Bedroom is a remarkable survival from the 1660s. It is the only bedroom in Britain where a balustrade still rails off the bed alcove from the rest of the room. This derives from the days when the British imitated the elaborate rituals of etiquette that regulated Louis XIV's court. At Versailles, when the monarch held his *leveé* (reception), only royal princes were allowed within the *ruelles* (spaces) on either side of the bed beyond the balustrade. The 1st Marquess would doubtless have used the room in much the same exclusive spirit in 1684, when his brother-in-law, the Duke of Beaufort, visited the castle during his progress as Lord President of Wales.

The balustrade may have been added by William Winde, probably in the 1680s, as it is more finely carved than the rest of the grained and gilded woodwork and similar to the 1680s balustrade of the Grand Staircase. It may also have been copied from the bed alcove at Greenwich Palace, designed in 1664–9 by John Webb.

The ubiquitous crowned CR cipher may commemorate Charles I, the Martyr King, or celebrate the Restoration of his son in 1660.

The visits of two kings are commemorated by the window latches in the shape of the Prince of Wales's feathers and by the elaborate gilt bronze door locks. The former record the visit of the future Edward VII. The future George V and Queen Mary stayed at Powis in 1909.

PICTURES

The ceiling painting shows *The Apotheosis of the Virgin and St Joseph*, and was adapted from a print after the French painter Simon Vouet (1590–1649). Over the chimneypiece is *The Adoration of the Shepherds* and, over the door, *The Resurrection*.

TAPESTRIES

The tapestries within the bed alcove, depicting the history of Alexander the Great, were woven in England in the 17th century and are from a larger set also represented at Sizergh Castle, Cumbria.

The 17th-century Brussels tapestries outside the bed alcove show Solomon and his concubines worshipping idols.

FURNITURE

The state bed of partly gilded mahogany is covered with crimson Spitalfields silk cut-velvet of *c.*1725, but only the inside of the canopy appears to be of this date. The rest of the bed (frame, posts and gilt cresting) is *c.*1780.

The silvered gesso sofa, chairs and stools are upholstered with the same velvet as the bed. There is an almost identical set of *c.*1725 at Erddig. They replaced a set upholstered in crimson velvet with gold fringes, seen here by Thomas Dineley in 1684.

The commode (chest-of-drawers) decorated with elaborate marquetry and with ormolu mounts is French, Louis XIV, *c.*1690.

The bracket clock in a Boulle (brass and tortoiseshell marquetry) case is signed by Etienne Collot – perhaps the François-Etienne Collot who was working in the Rue St Louis, Paris, in 1748. The case is surmounted by an ormolu figure of Juno, and the base is contemporary.

The walnut table veneered with floral marquetry is English, *c.*1690.

The rosewood and walnut display table contains a toilet set of gilded brass boxes with *champlevé* enamel, which is probably French, *c.*1685.

The carpet is Persian (Feraghan), 19th-century.

The enamelled toilet set is probably French, c.1685

(Right) The State Bedroom

THE LONG GALLERY

The Long Gallery is one of the most romantic of all rooms. Designed to connect the 'fairest Roomes' on the principal floor, its unusual 'T' shape causes a delightfully irregular play of light. It is also the only room decorated by Sir Edward Herbert between 1587 and 1595 to have remained intact. The elaborate plasterwork, the chimneypieces, the elm floor and the bizarre doorcase at the far end date from 1593. The *trompe-l'oeil* painted wainscot

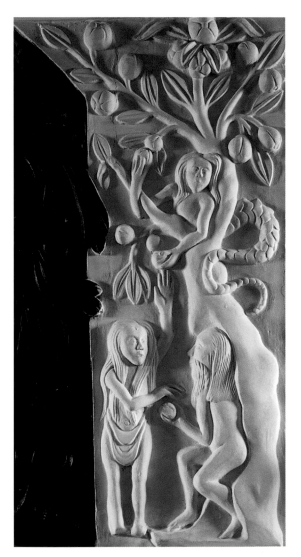

The 'Adam and Eve' plasterwork on the Long Gallery overmantel

was probably added early in the next century, and the 18th-century sashes replaced earlier stone windows.

HERALDRY

The gallery is emblazoned with the colourful devices of Sir Edward Herbert's ancestors. The coats of arms in the cornice frieze bear witness to generations of Herbert alliances, which are brought together over the central fireplace in Sir Edward's achievement of arms. Among the numerous quarterings are the Herbert arms: *per pale azure and gules, three lions rampant argent* surmounted by the wyvern crest: *A wyvern vert, holding in the mouth a sinister hand couped at the wrist gules*. On either side of this proud boast of heraldry appear Adam and Eve – surely an allusion to the antiquity of Sir Edward's pedigree. Above and to the right is the date 1593. Inside the chimney is a fireback with the arms of William, 1st Marquess of Powis (the earl's coronet dates it between 1674 and 1687) impaling the arms of Beaufort. Lord Powis was the brother-in-law of the Duke of Beaufort, who visited Powis in 1684 as Lord President of Wales.

PICTURES

Since 1684, travellers have remarked upon the family portraits, which Thomas Pennant in 1776 described as 'bad'.

9 *William Herbert, 3rd Earl of Pembroke (1580–1630)* by ABRAHAM VAN BLYENBERCH, 1617
Patron of Shakespeare, who dedicated the First Folio to him, and nephew of the first of the Herberts of Powis.

47 *Henry, 1st Earl of Powis (2nd creation) (1703–72)*, attributed to THOMAS HUDSON
He inherited Powis in 1748 from his distant cousin, the 3rd Marquess of Powis, and moved here permanently in 1771, when he was forced to sell his family's old home, Oakly Park, Ludlow, to pay his debts.

54 *Edward Herbert, 3rd Lord Herbert of Chirbury (1633–78)* by GERARD SOEST, c.1675
Great-uncle of 1st Earl (no. 47).

(Right) The Long Gallery

SCULPTURE

FROM STATE BEDROOM END:

The statue of a boy (with a girl's head) holding a dove in his right hand is a well known type, the so-called Eros of Centocelle, which is named after a marble now in the Vatican. It probably dates back to 4th-century Athens, and was imitated in a large number of Roman copies (at least 15 replicas are known). An original Pentelic (Roman or late Hellenistic) head of a little girl is attached to the ancient statue, via a modern neck made of Carrara marble, probably 18th-century.

Togatus with scroll in the typical manner of a Roman citizen, fashionable in the Imperial period. The single-strap boots are an indicator of status: the man is depicted as a Roman knight. The scroll in the Roman context is in general a mark of education. A standing togatus holding the scroll furthermore signifies a man with an important social position, either an advocate or politician, holding the manuscript of the speech he was about to give. The statue is probably 18th-century, made of Carrara marble. The small head should be regarded as a separate piece, a copy of a Vespasian-type, comparable to that of the colossal head of Vespasian found in Powis Castle among the twelve busts of the Caesars. Perhaps Clive of India chose this because he found there to be a slight resemblance to himself.

The statue of a boy holding a dove in his right hand is probably a figure of Eros, a popular memorial image for the tombs of boys and young men. The dove, an attribute of Venus, symbolises peace. The Parian marble face and torso are Roman, 1st- or 2nd-century AD; the remainder is Carrara marble, probably 18th-century.

FLANKING FIREPLACE ON RIGHT:

The bust of a goddess is probably intended to represent Isis, as the hairstyle is Egyptian. It is Neo-classical, 18th- or early 19th-century.

ON LEFT:

The bust of a goddess, its pendant, may represent Aphrodite, Greek goddess of love.

ON EAGLE TABLES:

The statue of a boy holding a pear is a copy after a Greek original of the 3rd century BC. The Hellenistic original is mostly known through small-scale terracotta figurines, in which the boy is easily identified as Hermes by the money-bag in his left hand. The form was reinterpreted in Roman times as a genre figure used for the funerary representation of boys. Thus the money-bag was replaced with various objects such as fruits or a cornucopia, with a pet such as a bird or dog held in the right hand. However, this Carrara marble statue must probably be regarded as the work of an 18th-century sculptor. Only the top of the tree trunk plus another two small pieces are original with the rest cleverly treated to look ancient.

The group of a Cat and Snake is Roman, 1st century BC–2nd century AD, probably derived from a lost Greek original. Representations of cats are rare in Roman art, and the Powis group is unique amongst surviving classical sculpture. It was made from the crystalline marble of Thasos, which is very difficult to work, but was valued for portrait sculpture and garden statuary because of its reflective qualities.

On 26 February 1774 Clive of India wrote from Rome to his wife, Margaret (who was fond of cats):

We have seen fine Churches, Statues and Pictures without Number and among other Curiosities, would you believe it an antique Cat. By the stile I should imagine it to be the work of some Grecian Artist for it is so exquisitely fine that no Roman statuary seems equal to such a Performance. You may imagine that I attempted to purchase it, I certainly did and can assure you was very lavish in my Offers for your sake, but alas I fear this delightful Cat is out of reach of Money, however I do not dispair and if I cannot succeed

(Left) Clive of India's cat

(Right) Statue symbolising water, Dutch, c.1700

whilst I am here I will leave Orders with my Agent to purchase the Cat if ever it is to be disposed of Coute qui coute [whatever the cost].

The baby with a dove in its left hand is a Carrara marble sculpture which could be considered as having an ancient torso. However, this is doubtful, in view of many inconsistencies, for example the atypical expression of happiness on the face. Such representations (children with their pets) were made exclusively as funerary depictions. The burial

marks appear realistic, but are also inconsistent so the statue is likely to be a good 18th-century forgery.

The five statues on the opposite side of the gallery are Dutch, early 18th-century, by the sculptor Peter van den Branden. They comprise the four elements (Earth, Air, Fire and Water), accompanied by Minerva (with the helmet and owl). A sixth figure of the goddess Juno, signed and dated 'van den Branden 1714', is in a private collection.

FURNITURE

FROM STATE BEDROOM END:

The circular-topped mosaic table is made up from antique fragments and may be one of the 'mosaic tables' designed by Robert Adam's teacher, Charles-Louis Clérisseau, in 1774 for Clive of India's villa, Claremont in Surrey.

The high-backed chairs, upholstered in green and original red velvet, are Dutch, in the manner of Daniel Marot, *c.*1730.

The day-bed covered in green velvet is English in the Restoration style, although made about 1830.

The walnut chest carved with a frieze of Renaissance medallions is French and is dated 1538.

The pietra dura table top was made in Florence c.1600

The gilt console tables with eagle supports and green marble tops are English, *c.*1730, and were at Powis House in London in 1772.

The ebony chairs were made in Sri Lanka. Such ebony furniture was avidly collected by 18th-century connoisseurs such as Horace Walpole, who believed they were English Elizabethan pieces.

The marble table in the cross gallery was made *c.*1600 in the *pietra dura* (hard stone) workshops set up in Florence by Grand Duke Ferdinand de' Medici in 1599, and was probably acquired by the 2nd Earl of Powis on his Grand Tour in 1775–6. The marble top is splendidly decorated with lapis lazuli, sardonyx, jasper, agate and other semi-precious stones. It is said to have come from the Borghese collection in Rome. In Italy, such tables usually had massive marble bases, which were often discarded by foreign collectors. The splendid wooden base of the Powis table appears to be contemporary with the top and is probably Italian.

The two chairs with painted leather upholstery are of oak, late 19th-century, in Cromwellian style.

The gilded brass wall-lights are *c.*1880–1900.

TAPESTRIES

The tapestries are from a fine 17th-century set of four (for a description, see p. 15). They depict (on the left) *Nebuchadnezzar warned* and (on the right) *The Golden Image*.

CLOCKS

The clock on the wall in the middle of the gallery is by Thomas Tompion, *c.*1680. The silvered face indicates four-hour intervals with a 'two minute' seconds dial and a 'ten minute' dial in the aperture above. It was used to test the accuracy of clocks and watches during manufacture. The plain oak workshop case has been veneered later with walnut set in ivory.

The longcase clock in the cross gallery is an eight-day regulator designed by Thomas Grignion of Covent Garden, London, and dated 1782.

(Right) Trompe l'oeil door and early 17th-century painted wainscot in the Long Gallery

The following four rooms, traditionally used by the family, are not always open.

THE STATE BATHROOM

When the State Bedroom was set up next door in the 1660s, this would have been a closet or ante-room for the sole use of the important guests who occupied it.

The fragment of panelling over the fireplace was probably removed from the Dining Room when Bodley remodelled that room in 1902.

THE WALCOT ROOM

This intimate room forms part of the family accommodation and differs in scale from the grandeur of the State Rooms. It was named after one of the family's other houses, Walcot Hall in Shropshire.

FURNITURE

The English oak bed is made from 17th-century carved panels decorated with primitive caryatids and Tudor roses. Bodley may have constructed it.

The built-in oak wardrobe was probably also made by Bodley.

THE GALLERY ROOM

This room, like the State Bathroom and Walcot Room, are formed in the thickness of the medieval curtain wall of the castle.

FURNITURE

The mahogany Empire secrétaire à abbatant (writing-desk), the chest-of-drawers and the dressing-table, all with ormolu mounts, are French, c.1810.

The walnut Hanseatic four-poster bed with panelled tester and carved headboard is German, c.1650s.

The Duke's Room

The bed-hangings and curtains are woven Jacquard brocade and were designed by Watts & Co. They were introduced by Bodley c.1902.

The Empire red griotte marble and ormolu clock flanked by bronze figures of Cupid and Psyche is French, c.1810.

The white marble bust of Napoleon was bought by Lord Clive, later 2nd Earl, from a dealer in Paris in 1814 for 15s.

THE DUKE'S ROOM

This room is named after William, 2nd Marquess and titular Duke of Powis (c.1665–1745), who used it as a bedroom. It was remodelled about 1902 by Bodley, who retained the fine late Elizabethan plasterwork ceiling.

FURNITURE

The four-poster bed, c.1600–10, has a heavily carved and inlaid tester and headboard decorated with caryatid figures and 17th-century crewelwork hangings. It came from the Herberts' house at Lymore in Montgomeryshire.

The inlaid walnut cabinet veneered with marquetry is English, c.1680–90.

The comfortable armchairs are covered with Watts & Co.'s 'Memlinc' fabric.

TEXTILES

The needlework carpet with panels of roses is c.1790.

The 17th-century Brussels tapestries illustrate *The Court of King Solomon*, *The Rape of the Sabine Women* and *The Meeting of Esau and Jacob*. They come from a set formerly at Lymore.

THE LOWER TOWER BEDROOM

This was one of the 6th Earl of Powis's guest bedrooms.

PICTURES

The overmantel dates from c.1700. On the wall to the right there are two small oval portraits after Hugh Douglas Hamilton of *Sir Henry Strachey*

G. F. Bodley designed this neo-Jacobean doorcase for the Duke's Room as part of his remodelling of the castle in 1902–4

and *Caroline Stuart, Duchess of Albany*. They were framed to match those in the Blue Drawing Room.

FURNITURE AND TEXTILES

The mahogany tester bed, c.1760s, has finely carved Gothick posts and a delicate close-covered fretwork cresting. The coverlet is a Mughal floor-spread, c.1700, embroidered in silver and silver-gilt thread and probably from the Clive collection.

The curious kneehole desk of beech, c.1720, beyond the bed incorporates fragments of Indian inlay in a chequered pattern of ivory and ebony.

The large walnut cupboard to the right of the door was probably made up from older Dutch marquetry panels in the late 19th century.

THE GRAND STAIRCASE

The great stairway leading up to the first-floor State Rooms was commissioned between 1674 and 1687 by William, 1st Marquess of Powis, whose coat of arms is displayed (above the landing) at the foot of the ceiling painting. The superb carved door-cases and inlaid stair treads are attributed to William Winde.

CEILING PAINTING

The Italian artist Antonio Verrio (c.1639–97) painted the ceiling in the 1670s. He had come to England in 1672 and established a large practice, inspiring Alexander Pope's lines:

On painted ceilings you devoutly stare
Where sprawl the Saints of *Verrio* and *Laguerre*,
On gilded clouds in fair expansion lie,
And bring all Paradise before your Eye.

The Powis ceiling may represent the coronation of Charles II's queen, Catherine of Braganza, whose Catholic faith was shared by Lord Powis. Certainly, the figure wearing a red tunic and crowned with laurels seated on a cloud to the left of the queen

The Triumph of Neptune and Amphitrite; *mural by Gerard Lanscroon*

bears a distinct resemblance to Charles II, and the royal CR cipher appears below. The composition is adapted from Veronese's *Apotheosis of Venice* (1553–5) in the Doge's Palace, Venice.

WALL PAINTINGS

In 1705 Lord Powis's son, the 2nd Marquess, commissioned Verrio's pupil Gerard Lanscroon (active 1677–d.1737) to paint the walls of the staircase. Lord Powis's monogram and ducal coronet is borne up by deities high on the left-hand wall above a scene representing *Vulcan forging the arms of Achilles*. On the right wall is the *Triumph of Neptune and Amphitrite*, together with the *Three Fates*, *Ceres*, *Apollo*, *Painting* and *History*.

RESTORATION

Both ceiling and wall-paintings have recently been conserved with support from the Historic Buildings Council of Wales and the Council of Museums in Wales. This entailed removing old discoloured repaint which had been added in the past to hide cracks caused by subsidence.

A 'large sash window' was replaced by Bodley c.1902–4, who installed the armorial glass which illustrates the 4th Earl's descent from Clive of India.

CONTENTS

The late 15th-century broadsword on the wall by the door leading from the Long Gallery is traditionally associated with the Lords President of Wales, who held court between 1478 and 1689 at Ludlow Castle, which is owned by the Earls of Powis.

Roman statue of a Muse, Demeter- (or Ceres-) type set upon a funerary altar was made up in the 18th century from a probably Italian 1st or 2nd century AD body and a different head; the right arm and left hand are 18th-century replacements. It is probably the piece bought by Clive of India in Rome in March 1774, which he thought was 'one of the most delightful pleasing Statues I ever saw'. The funerary altar is a fine example of c.AD 100 formerly in the Mattei Collection in Rome. The altar has been let into a modern plinth with a relief of a sacrificial jug, after the Roman manner, carved on the side. The tree flanked by birds is an olive; the garlands are suspended from ram's heads, and there are sphinxes projecting below. All these are conventional elements of funerary art.

(Right) The Grand Staircase

The Blue Drawing Room

THE BLUE DRAWING ROOM

The design of the panelling is very similar to that of the State Bedroom, which suggests a date in the 1660s, when this would have been used as the Great Chamber or Saloon. The room has changed little since 1705, when Lanscroon painted the ceiling, which probably represents *Peace banishing War from the Four Continents*. In 1752 it was used as a drawing room, but had become a dining room by 1772.

Bodley probably supplied the blue and gold 'Memlinc' curtain material, which is a Watts & Co. pattern. The blue scheme dates from the 1930s, when E. Guy Dawber redecorated the room.

PICTURES

8 *Lady Elizabeth Somerset, Marchioness of Powis* (*c.*1633–91) by JOHN MICHAEL WRIGHT
She accompanied her husband, the 1st Marquess of Powis, into exile in 1688, when she served as Governess of the Royal Children.

61 *Mary Preston, Marchioness of Powis* (d.1724), attributed to CHARLES D'AGAR
Daughter-in-law of no. 8.

68 *The Madonna and Child*, attributed to BRESCIANINO (active 1507–25)

102–13 *Oval portraits of the 1st and 2nd Earls of Powis (3rd creation) and their relations* by HUGH DOUGLAS HAMILTON and ANNA TONELLI
Framed together. Hamilton painted the 1st Earl and his family while they were in Rome in 1788. Tonelli taught drawing to the 1st Earl's children.

TAPESTRIES

The three tapestries are from a set of four depicting the story of Julius Caesar: *The Surrender of Cleopatra, The Death of Pompey* and *Attack on a Fortress*. They are signed by Marcus de Vos, one of the principal weavers in late 17th-century Brussels.

FURNITURE

The carved and gilt suite of sofa and chairs is covered in blue and gold 'Memlinc' damask designed by Bodley and made by Watts & Co. The suite was in the Drawing Room at 45 Berkeley Square, the town house of the Earls of Powis until 1937. It was probably commissioned by Clive of India, who altered and furnished the house in 1766/7.

The sofa table decorated with rustic scenes in marquetry is from Sorrento in Italy, *c.*1825–50.

LACQUER FURNITURE

The pair of commodes with ormolu mounts is attributed to Pierre Langlois, a French craftsman with a shop in London whose lacquer and inlaid furniture was fashionable in the 1760s. Commodes of this quality were intended for display rather than use. The lacquer is Chinese and was once part of a screen.

The pair of knife-boxes standing on the commodes is Japanese, *c.*1725–50, their lacquer is of exceptionally high quality.

The six-fold screen is Chinese, late 17th-century, with English mounts, *c.*1715, and probably depicts scenes from a novel.

The pair of boxes on English cabriole leg stands is Japanese, *c.*1730. 'Two japan dressing boxes' are listed in Clive of India's collection, but the shape of these dressing-cum-writing boxes suggests an earlier date, and they may have been ordered by the 2nd Marquess of Powis (*c.*1665–1745). Japanese unfamiliarity with dressing-tables may explain why the boxes have lacquer panels instead of mirrors fixed above.

The square cabinet-on-stand is Japanese, *c.*1695. The stand is English, mid-18th-century.

The set of 'Quartetto' tables is from Canton, *c.*1820. Small tables made in graduated sizes to fit one below the other are called 'quartetto' tables because there are four in a set. According to George Smith's *Household Furniture* (1808), they 'prevent the company rising from their seats, when taking refreshments'.

The lacquer boxes on the table are Japanese, *c.*1700.

CLOCKS

The Boulle pedestal and bracket clocks with ormolu mounts are French, *c.*1730.

MISCELLANEOUS

The silver wall-lights bearing the arms of the 2nd Marquess of Powis are copies by G. Fox, 1904.

The large enamel dish, decorated with scenes from Genesis, is signed 'P.R.' for Pierre Reymond (*c.*1513–after 1567), one of a family of Limoges enamellers.

The enamel bowl and cover is also signed by Reymond. The ormolu mounts are probably French, *c.*1750.

TEXTILES

The carpet is Persian (Feraghan), 19th-century. Until 1937, it was in the Drawing Room at 45 Berkeley Square, London.

Descend the servants' staircase, passing the entrance to the Old Kitchen on the right at the foot of the stairs. The passage to the courtyard leads past the servants' quarters and the corridor to the wine and beer cellars (on the left).

(Left) One of a pair of commodes by Pierre Langlois

THE BILLIARD ROOM

When the domestic offices were moved from the main castle in 1772, this room became the Servants' Hall, and was used as such until the present century. As its original furniture and fittings had long disappeared, it was converted into a billiard room in 1986. The billiard table by Burroughs & Watts and the cases of stuffed birds were formerly in the old billiard room of 1902–4 in the Ballroom range, which is now part of the Clive Museum.

STUFFED BIRDS

The ornithological collection may include specimens brought back from India by Henrietta, wife of the 2nd Lord Clive (1758–1830), but most of the birds date from c.1850. The taxidermy and the construction of the oak cases were probably undertaken by Henry Shaw (1812–87) of 45, The High Street, Shrewsbury. Shaw's reputation was considerable, and the Dukes of Portland and Westminster were among his clients.

THE BILLIARD ROOM PASSAGE

This passage is hung with 19th- and early 20th-century illuminated addresses presented to the Earls of Powis by their tenants. The fire-engine is 18th-century, and by the door into the courtyard there is a collection of 19th-century firefighting apparatus.

Visitors cross the castle courtyard and enter the Ballroom on the right.

THE BALLROOM STAIRCASE

At the foot of the stairs is a photograph of Edward, 3rd Earl of Powis (1818–91). The vicious mantraps on the adjoining wall are a reminder of the risks run by 18th- and 19th-century poachers.

THE BALLROOM

In 1776 George, 2nd Earl of Powis celebrated his 21st birthday in this room, which he had commissioned two years before from Thomas Farnolls Pritchard of Shrewsbury. The new ballroom replaced a long gallery that was separated from the main castle by a fire c.1725.

The entrance to the Ballroom is beneath a musicians' gallery supported by the attenuated columns that are a trademark of Pritchard's style. The stucco capitals and frieze are of the fine quality that Pritchard's plasterer, Joseph Bromfield, achieved at Attingham Park and Oakly Park, Ludlow. The room was originally painted green, with the ornamental plasterwork picked out in white. Although the formal dances of the 18th century demanded a long rectangular room, the Powis ballroom seemed narrow even to a contemporary eye. Henry Skrine wrote in 1798 that 'its breadth is very disproportionate to its length and gives it the appearance of a gallery'.

Bodley shortened the Ballroom in 1902–4: the break in the ceiling plasterwork can be clearly seen at the far end. Bodley also replaced the 18th-century sash-windows with the present mullions.

PICTURES

Clive of India's famous collection of Old Master pictures was moved by his son to Powis for safekeeping on the latter's departure for India in 1798. By 1816 the collection was moved to Walcot in Shropshire, the seat of the Earl of Powis, whose eldest son, Viscount Clive, was the owner of Powis Castle. When Walcot was sold with most of its

(Left) An embassy to Constantinople; detail of the tapestry in the Ballroom

The Ballroom

contents by the 4th Earl of Powis in 1929, some paintings from the collection returned to Powis.

5 *Margaret Maskelyne, Lady Clive* (1733–1817) by ? NATHANIEL DANCE
Wife of Clive of India and a great lover of music: hence the score on the table.

69 *Lady Lucy Graham, Countess of Powis* (1793–1875) by Sir FRANCIS GRANT
Her marriage to the 2nd Earl (no. 70) in 1818 was celebrated with a huge party for the tenantry.

70 *Edward Herbert, 2nd Earl of Powis* (1785–1848) by Sir FRANCIS GRANT
Commissioned Sir Robert Smirke to repair the castle in the early 19th century.

73 *A Chestnut Stallion in the grounds of Powis Castle* by JAMES WARD, 1818

79 *Landscape with Huntsman and Dead Game* by JAN WEENIX, 16?9
Bought by Clive of India in 1771.

114 *Lord Clive receiving the grant of the diwani from the Great Mogul* by BENJAMIN WEST
On 12 August 1765 the Mughal Emperor Shah Allam II conferred the fiscal administration (or *diwani*) of Bengal, Behar and Orissa on Clive of India. On loan from the British Library.

FURNITURE

The giltwood chandeliers are English, c.1900, in the Georgian style.

The bookcases, c.1795, of mahogany inlaid with satinwood, were transferred from Walcot Hall in 1929.

The grand piano by John Broadwood & Sons is numbered 18389, which dates it to 1854/5. Alec Cobbe presented it to the National Trust in 1983.

TEXTILES

The magnificent tapestry, the most important in the castle, is dated 1545 and was probably woven in Tournai. It depicts an embassy to Constantinople probably by the Fleming Weltwyck, who, on behalf of the Emperor Charles V and Ferdinand, King of Hungary, secured a treaty with Suleiman the Magnificent in 1547. The tapestry came from Lymore, near Chirbury, the former seat of the Lords Herbert of Chirbury.

CERAMICS

The Imari vases on top of the bookcases are Japanese, c.1700, and were possibly acquired by Clive of India.

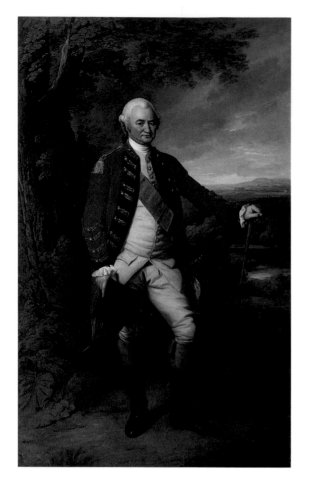

THE CLIVE MUSEUM

This room was set up in 1987 in the former billiard room. The Neo-classical fireplace and the plaster arabesques visible on the walls betray the fact that this space was part of the Ballroom until Bodley truncated it in 1902–4, adding a mezzanine floor.

The collection of weapons, ivories, textiles and ornamental silver and gold brought from India by Robert Clive was first kept at his Surrey home, Claremont, but with the addition of pieces collected by his son Edward and the latter's wife Henrietta Herbert it seems to have been bought to Powis at the very end of the 18th century. There are now over 300 items of Indian and Far Eastern origin, ranging in date from the 17th to the 19th centuries. The museum was opened in July 1987 by the Countess Mountbatten of Burma. In 1999 many of the items on display were acquired with the support of the National Heritage Memorial Fund and the National Art Collections Fund.

The Clive Museum was designed by Alec Cobbe, the display cases made by Sussex cabinet-maker John Hart. Their design and decorations are intended to recall the architecture of India as translated into English settings, such as Brighton Pavilion.

(Left) Robert Clive of India; by Nathaniel Dance (no. 33; Oak Drawing Room). His son married the last of the Powis Herberts and brought the Clive collections to the castle

The hilt of Tipu Sultan's sword

(Left) The Clive Museum

Maharaja Pratap Singh of Tangore

THE COACH HOUSE

The Coach House has been adapted to provide an environmentally sound setting for this fragile but magnificent equipage – the finest in the ownership of the National Trust, together with the associated liveries and an ornate harness that would have been placed on a horse armature.

The State Coach was used in London by the Earls of Powis for occasions of state, court functions or when engaged on the most formal of business matters. Except possibly for very important family occasions such as weddings, they would have been completely out of place on country roads. It is rare for the accompanying harness and liveries to survive too. Other carriages, of varying degrees of formality, would have been used for everyday travel.

HARNESS

The splendid harnes is embellished with the Earl's coat of arms, crest and coronet, all in silver-plate. A matching pair of elegant and powerful horses would have been used to pull the coach. The coach has no brakes, so the horses took the weight through the breeching straps round the hind quarters. This type of coach was only suitable for use in London streets; the Earls of Powis had a town house in Berkeley Square.

LIVERIES

All aristocratic families had a distinctive uniform, or livery, for their servants. On formal occasions there would have been a coachman and two footmen. The coachman, employed for his equestrian skills, would wear a white wig and tricorn hat, the foot-

The Miseries of London *by Rowlandson, 1807. This satirical cartoon comments upon the miseries of traffic congestion, experienced by Regency commuters (Caricature Room at Calke Abbey, also a National Trust property)*

(Above) The State Coach

men, more decorative, wore cocked hats and stood on the back, carrying silver-topped staves, known as wands, originally used to protect the passengers from assailants.

Hand-written labels inside the coats show that these liveries were supplied in 1898, for the 4th Earl of Powis. They were made by London tailors, Rimmell & Allsop of New Bond Street, for a coachman by the name of Mills, and for his colleagues, footmen Welland and Wright. Mills later went on to become the family's chauffeur.

THE STATE COACH

The coach was built by Wyburn & Co. of London, one of the leading carriage builders of the day, for the 3rd Earl of Powis, who inherited the title in 1848. The coach is decorated with the family coat of arms on the doors and the crest on the panels.

The trimmings are of the highest quality, the external metalwork being silver-plated rather than brass.

INTERIOR

For conservation reasons, the coach is not shown open (an illustration of the interior is on display).

The interior of the coach is upholstered in buttercup yellow corded silk and tan Morocco leather. The doors are each fitted with a glass window which can be pulled up manually by a silk-tasselled strap. A panel blind, designed to imitate a Venetian blind, rests on the rail alongside the ornate door-handle. A further roller blind, of crimson taffeta, is fitted on the inside above the door.

A single tassel hanging from the roof of the coach links to a silk cord. This was attached to the coachman's finger and was the sole means of communication between passengers and driver.

THE GARDEN AND PARK

Powis is justly famous for its terraced garden, which provides such a dramatic frame for the south front of the castle. Conceived in the 1680s for the 1st Marquess of Powis, it is one of the few baroque gardens to have survived in more or less its original form. After periods of neglect, it was revived by Violet, Countess of Powis in 1911.

THE BAROQUE GARDEN

The design of the Powis terraces has been attributed to the gentleman-architect Captain William Winde, who was the godson of the 1st Marquess's uncle. Captain Winde was a military engineer and so would have known how to blast the terraces out of the solid rock, if they did not already exist. He probably also created the similar terraced garden at

(Below) Bird's-eye view of the terraced garden in 1741; by Samuel and Nathaniel Buck

Cliveden in Buckinghamshire and was certainly the architect of the 1st Marquess's London house in 1684–8 (see p. 44).

Work on the Powis garden stopped in 1688, when the 1st Marquess fled to France with his deposed King, James II. The exiled court settled near Paris at the château of St Germain-en-Laye, where the great French garden designer André le Nôtre had created a famous terraced garden embellished with niches, parterres and waterworks very similar to those once at Powis. It was the French who introduced the idea of the terraced garden to northern Europe from Italy, where it had been invented in the 16th century.

Although Winde visited Powis in 1697, work on the garden does not seem to have started again until 1703, when the 2nd Marquess returned from exile, bringing with him a French gardener, Adrian Duval – probably the 'de Valle' whom the antiquary John Loveday believed was responsible for creating

A niche on the Top Terrace

the terraces. Duval may also have designed the elaborate water garden that lay below the terraces on what is now the Grand Lawn and which so impressed John Bridgeman in 1705: 'The water-works and fountains that are finished there are much beyond anything I ever saw whose streams play near twenty yards in height the Cascade has too falls of water which concludes in a noble Bason.' Payments to Duval in 1713 and 1717 suggest that work continued for many years.

A bird's-eye view published by Samuel and Nathaniel Buck in 1741 shows the baroque garden in its prime. The balustraded terraces, the brick orangery and open arcades designed to catch the best of the southern sun still survive immediately below the castle, but the neatly clipped yew bushes recorded by the Bucks on either side have since swelled hugely and subsided out of shape. The flat ground below was divided into three parterres with formal pools and statues in the centre edged with more topiary. The Bucks' view does not show the cascade that probably ran down the slope facing the castle, but Loveday described it in 1736:

The Water-works in ys Garden are finer than I have seen elsewhere; several Leaden Cisterns, one lower than another, like so many Stairs, when Water is convey'd into ye first, make a noble Cascade; Stone Basons or Cisterns also, on each side down ye Descent are with the same design. Higher than this, an open Room, where are Shells set in regular figures in ye Wall.

The many lead statues and urns that still ornament the terraces were an attractive advertisement for the family's lead mines in Montgomeryshire, which helped to rescue its finances in the early 18th century (see p. 46). The huge lead statues of *Fame* (now in the entrance courtyard) and of *Hercules* on the top terrace were made by Andries Carpentière, a key craftsman in the workshop of John van Nost, who also provided statuary for Powis House, the family's London home. If left unprotected out of doors, lead sculpture will corrode and so it was traditionally painted, either in naturalistic colours or to resemble more prestigious stone sculpture.

(Left) A lead statue from the workshop of John van Nost

DECLINE

A survey by Thomas Farnolls Pritchard in 1771 shows a lozenge-shaped plantation on the site of the present Upper Lawn with straight paths converging on a central round pond with another large fountain. But by 1771 the parterres had disappeared from the water garden, and much of the other formal planting had been simplified. In that year the landscape designer William Emes was consulted about new planting in the Wilderness – the informal woodland which has always occupied the ridge facing the castle and complements the

(Above) The Orangery Terrace

(Right) The Bodley gates were commissioned by Violet, Lady Powis in 1912 as part of her revival of the garden

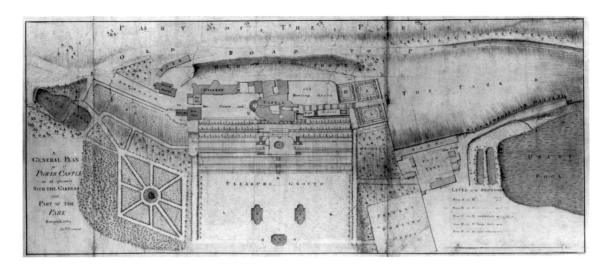

The garden in 1771; survey by T. F. Pritchard

formality of the terraces opposite. In 1778 Emes also supplied designs for greenhouses in which to grow vines and peaches.

When Lord Torrington visited Powis in 1784, the garden was in a sorry state: 'Not even the fruit is attended to; the balustrades and terraces are falling down, and horses graze on the parterres!!!' By 1793, things had got even worse: 'Upon the terraces you cannot walk as the balustrades are fallen down; and should you slip you are lost.' The landscape theorist Richard Payne Knight helped to ensure that the terraces were not swept away, and drawings made by J. C. Buckler in 1822 show the terrace planting had been renewed with ornamental shrubs, trees and climbers. Where the pools had once been, deer grazed in open parkland.

THE 20TH CENTURY

In September 1911 Violet, Countess of Powis decided to take the garden properly in hand: 'I have a great task before me. There is so much to undo, so much to do, and to plan.' Her aim was to make the garden 'one of the most beautiful if not the most beautiful in England and Wales'. She concentrated on the area to the east of the Grand Lawn, which was occupied by the decaying remains of the 18th-century kitchen garden: 'I see velvet lawns and

wide paths: rose gardens – fountains – clipped yews – marble seats – herbaceous borders.' The Edwardian garden that she created was entirely new, but it drew on the example of the original baroque design. So, for instance, in 1912 she commissioned new wrought-iron gates from G. F. Bodley for her garden based on those that once fronted Powis House. They have been recently restored with funds from the Worshipful Company of Ironmongers. She also much enriched the planting on the terraces, a process continued by the Trust.

THE PARK

The local climate and soil make Powis an ideal place in which to grow trees. There has been a wooded deer-park here since the Middle Ages, and some of the ancient oaks, beeches and sycamores date back to the 16th century. A drawing made by Thomas Dineley in 1684 suggests that some of the park was then planted in the same formal manner as the baroque garden, with a straight avenue leading up to the east front of the castle.

Many conifers were planted in the 18th century, when the family was often short of money and the park was treated as commercial forestry. In 1771 Emes was consulted about new planting and roads in the park, but most of the older trees date from the first half of the 19th century, when the park was renewed after years of neglect.

LIFE AT POWIS

MEDIEVAL POWIS

In the 12th century, the kingdom of Powys was already known as 'the paradise of Wales'. Famous for its mild climate, fertile soil and gently rolling hills, it covered the south-eastern half of north Wales. But it was in a vulnerable position, sandwiched between more powerful neighbours – the Welsh kingdom of Gwynedd to the north-west, and England over the nearby border to the east. If Powys was to survive, it had to side with one or the other.

The great warrior-poet Owain Cyfeiliog, Prince of southern Powys from 1160 to 1197, was at home in English court circles, swapping jokes with Henry II over supper at Shrewsbury. He was probably responsible for moving the capital of southern Powys from its ancient seat at Mathrafal nine miles east to Welshpool, which soon became a thriving commercial centre with strong trading links with England down the Severn valley. He may also, in the late 12th century, have begun the present castle, which, for some reason, has always been spelt 'Powis'. It follows the conventional Norman layout, with a strong keep (the present castle), an inner bailey (the entrance courtyard) and a massive outer wall (the Ballroom range). It was built from the craggy outcrop of red gritstone on which it stands – hence its Welsh name 'Y Castell Coch' ('The Red Castle').

Owain's overtures towards England did him little good. In 1196, an English army under Archbishop Hubert Walter marched up the Severn, laid siege to the castle and captured it. Owain died the following year a beaten man. His son, Gwenwynwyn ap Owain, adopted a very different strategy. As soon as he inherited, he took on the mantle of Wales's deliverer from the English and began expanding his kingdom, but his ambitions were crushed almost immediately. On 13 August 1198 at the Battle of Painscastle his army was annihilated by the English.

He tried to re-establish his authority, but in 1208 was forced to surrender to King John at Shrewsbury, where he recovered his lands only at the cost of a very public humiliation. Gwenwynwyn had also provoked the jealous rivalry of Llywelyn ab Iorwerth of Gwynedd, the most powerful of all the Welsh lords, who himself coveted the title of Prince of Wales. In 1216, Llywelyn invaded Powys, driving out Gwenwynwyn, who died shortly afterwards in exile in England.

Gwenwynwyn's son Gruffudd took to heart the unhappy fates of his father and grandfather. He realised that he would have to be both more modest in his ambitions and cunning in his methods, if he were to get Powys back. He also had to be patient, only coming in to his inheritance on the death of Llywelyn in 1240 and thanks to the support of the English king. Llywelyn's grandson and successor, Llywelyn ap Gruffudd, continued the feud between Gwynedd and Powys, driving Gruffudd into exile again in 1257–63 and 1274–77. To recover his kingdom in 1263, Gruffudd swore oaths of submission to Llywelyn. In 1277 he decided to support Edward I, when he invaded Wales in order to crush Llywelyn ap Gruffudd, who was now in open rebellion against the English crown. Edward's victory marked the end of Welsh resistance to English authority until Owain Glyn Dŵr's rebellion of 1400–10, but it did at least return Gruffudd to Powis. Gruffudd rebuilt the castle, which had been badly damaged during Llywelyn's siege of 1274, and died secure in his kingdom in 1286.

Gruffud's son, Owain, was the last Prince of Powys, paying homage to Edward I and entering Parliament with the Norman title Baron de la Pole (ie of Pool, or Powis, Castle). He was probably responsible for building most of what we see today around 1300, including the two drum towers that

The drum towers which guard the entrance survive from the medieval castle

overlook the entrance courtyard. His nineteen-year-old daughter, Hawys, continued the work after she inherited the castle in 1309, but her right to it was disputed by her uncle, who besieged Powis in 1312. Hawys held out, and such was her courage in defending the castle that she gained the nickname 'y Gadarn' ('the Hardy'). Her husband, who was created Lord Cherleton of Powis, was one of the most powerful of the feudal Lords of the Welsh Marches. Powis passed by direct descent to Edward,

5th and last feudal Lord Cherleton, who remained loyal to the English Crown, when his Welsh tenants backed the rebellion of Owain Glyn Dŵr in 1401. The castle was besieged, and the English inhabitants of Welshpool massacred, but again Powis held out. After the rebellion had been crushed, Cherleton obtained a royal pardon for those of his Welsh tenants who had followed Glyn Dŵr.

Cherleton had no sons, and so on his death in 1421 Powis was divided between his two daughters. In 1578 a descendant of the elder daughter leased the castle to Sir Edward Herbert, who had taken full possession by 1587. A new family brought a new life to Powis.

A NEW FAMILY

SIR EDWARD HERBERT
(c.1542–95)

Sir Edward Herbert was a second son. While his elder brother inherited the family's Wilton estate in Wiltshire, he had to make his own way in the world. He had good reason for choosing to settle at Powis, for his family had had Welsh connections since at least the 14th century, when they had acquired property in Monmouthshire. Sir Edward's grandfather had been created Earl of Pembroke by Edward IV in 1468, and the title had been revived for his father by Henry VIII, whose sixth queen, Catherine Parr, was Sir Edward's aunt. There were also Herbert kinsmen not far away at Montgomery Castle and over the border at Chirbury.

Between 1587 and his death in 1595, Sir Edward Herbert made extensive improvements to the castle, but all that survives of this work is the atmospheric Long Gallery, which is dated 1593. Such rooms were often built in Elizabethan houses to display family portraits. At Powis, Sir Edward chose to celebrate his ancient lineage with a plasterwork frieze, which is decorated with the coats of arms of his ancestors supported by fabulous beasts. The Herberts' Catholic tradition seems to have begun with Sir Edward and his wife, Mary Stanley.

WILLIAM, 1ST LORD POWIS
(1574–1656)

Sir Edward's son William inherited Powis at the age of 21, and it was to be his home for the next tumultuous half-century. He married a fellow-

(Right)
The first Lord Herbert of Chirbury by Peake, in his 'robes of crimson taffety' described in his autobiography (no. 26; Oak Drawing Room)

(Above) William, 1st Lord Powis, whose estates were confiscated in 1644 for his support of Charles I during the Civil War (no. 12; Dining Room)

*(Right)
Eleanor Percy,
who married
the 1st Lord
Powis (no. 11;
Dining Room)*

*(Far right)
? Elizabeth
Spencer, the
wife of Lord
Craven, the
brother-in-law
of the 2nd Lord
Powis (no. 38;
Gateway Room)*

Catholic, Lady Eleanor Percy, the daughter of the 8th Earl of Northumberland, who had been executed for plotting with Mary, Queen of Scots against Queen Elizabeth. Lady Eleanor inherited a wooden rosary that had belonged to the Scottish Queen, which is displayed in the Gateway Room.

In 1629 William Herbert was created 1st Lord Powis by Charles I, and he loyally supported the King throughout the Civil War. On 2 October 1644 the castle was captured by Parliamentary troops under the command of Sir Thomas Myddelton of nearby Chirk Castle (now also the property of the National Trust):

At two of the clock even by moonlight, Mr John Arundell, the master gunner to Sir Thomas Middleton, placed a petard [explosive charge] against the outer gate, which burst the gate quite in pieces, and (notwithstanding the many showers of stones thrown from the castle by the enemy) Sir Thomas Middleton's foote, commanded by Captain Hugh Massey and Major Henry Kett, rushed with undaunted resolution into the enemy's works, got into the porch of the castle, and so stormed the castle gate, entered it and possessed themselves of the old and the new castle, and of all the plate, provisions, and goods therein (which was a great store).

Lord Powis's estates were all confiscated, and by now 'infirm and weake', he was reduced to living on £4 a week in lodgings in London. He died in 1656 without ever regaining Powis, which was occupied by a Parliamentary committee.

PERCY, 2ND LORD POWIS
(c.1598–1667)

The 1st Baron's son Percy was equally devoted to the Royalist cause, but fell out with his father, who accused him of disloyalty. He had married Elizabeth Craven, the sister of the 1st Earl of Craven, who had built Ashdown House in Oxfordshire (also the property of the National Trust) and was the most faithful supporter of Charles I's sister, the tragic 'Winter Queen' of Bohemia. In 1651 he was convicted of treason by Parliament, stripped of all his estates, and sent to prison. He wrote a remarkably philosophical reflection on his fate, entitled *Certaine Conceptions or Considerations of Sir Percy Herbert upon the strange change of people's dispositions and actions in these latter times*. When he was freed, he seems to have lived at Buttington near Welshpool, but may have begun restoring the dilapidated castle.

MAKING A BAROQUE PALACE

WILLIAM, 1ST MARQUESS OF POWIS
(c.1626–96)

William Herbert had a dramatically changing career at the centre of national life, rising and falling more than once with the twists and turns of Stuart politics. Through all the ups and downs, he steadily transformed Powis from a medieval castle into a mansion fit for a great nobleman.

As soon as he inherited Powis in 1667, he began creating a palatial State Apartment within the castle walls – in what is now the Blue Drawing Room and Library. It climaxed at the opposite end of the Long Gallery in the State Bedroom, which is laid out on the very formal pattern devised by French royalty, with a four-poster bed set in an alcove behind a balustrade. Herbert was probably encouraged to transform Powis in this way by his brother-in-law, the 1st Duke of Beaufort, who enjoyed at

Badminton 'a princely way of living … above any other, except crowned heads'. In 1684 the Duke dined in splendour at Powis and then slept in the State Bedroom during his progress as Lord President of Wales. If Lord Powis had hoped that his new apartments would one day also welcome the King, he was disappointed. However, Charles II did bestow an earldom on him in 1674. To celebrate his elevation, the 1st Earl created the Grand Staircase and had it decorated with a vast allegorical ceiling painting by the greatest exponent of the style, Antonio Verrio, which may represent the coronation of Charles II's queen, Catherine of Braganza.

The 1st Earl was a Catholic, but was careful not to antagonise the Protestant majority and to profess his loyalty to the Crown. However, in 1678 he was named by Titus Oates as a conspirator in the 'Popish Plot' to kill Charles II and replace him with his Catholic younger brother, James, Duke of York. Although these accusations were entirely invented, the 1st Earl was imprisoned in the Tower of London for five years. When he was released in 1684, he and his family were lucky to escape with their lives, when their London house was burnt to the ground by an anti-Catholic mob. He at once commissioned William Winde, who may have designed the terraces at Powis, to build him a grand new town house in Lincoln's Inn Fields.

The following year, James became King, and Lord Powis's fortunes rose once more. He became a member of the Privy Council and was created 1st Marquess of Powis. He tried to restrain James II from adopting a too overtly Catholic policy, but failed. When, as a result, James was driven from the throne in 1688, he helped the Prince of Wales to escape and loyally followed the King into exile at St Germain-en-Laye near Paris, where he served as Comptroller of the Household and his wife Elizabeth as Governess of the Royal Children. James rewarded him for his devotion with a Dukedom in 1689, but, not surprisingly, this was not recognised by William III's new regime, which had confiscated his estates. When Lord Powis died in exile in 1696, James's queen, Mary of Modena, remarked, 'My partner has lost a most honest, zealous servant; and I a most faithful friend'.

*(Above) Elizabeth, Marchioness of Powis,
who served as Governess of the Royal Children;
by J. M. Wright (no. 8; Blue Drawing Room)*

*(Above, right) Lady Mary Herbert,
daughter of the 1st Marquess; painted
by François de Troy c.1686–96, when
she was in exile in France with her
parents (no. 65; Dining Room)*

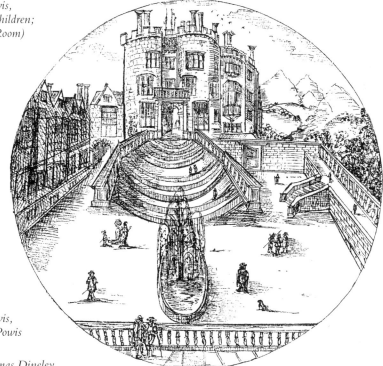

*(Far left) William, 1st Marquess of Powis,
who created palatial new apartments at Powis
and followed James II into exile in 1688*

(Right) The courtyard in 1684; by Thomas Dineley

WILLIAM, 2ND MARQUESS OF POWIS
(*c.*1665–1745)

The 2nd Marquess inherited his father's original title in 1696, but, as the son of a traitor, remained under suspicion and endured periods of imprisonment and exile between 1697 and 1701, and again during the Jacobite rising of 1715. In 1696 William III granted most of the Powis estates to his nephew, William van Zuylesteyn, who was created Earl of Rochford. Rochford received the estate rents, and all the goods and chattels in the castle, but seems never to have lived here, allowing the Marquess to return in 1703.

The 2nd Marquess continued his father's work on the castle, commissioning murals for the Grand Staircase from Lanscroon and another painted ceiling featuring his daughters for the Library in 1705, building the Marquess Gate in 1707, and completing the terraced gardens. He also built a new London house in Great Ormond Street. He could afford to do all this only because in 1692 a rich vein of lead ore had been discovered at Llangynog, which his lawyers managed to keep out of Lord Rochford's hands by settling the property on trustees. Full-scale development of the lead mine began in 1705, but the family's new-found wealth was threatened by the 2nd Marquess's daughter, Lady Mary Herbert. She began recklessly

Lanscroon's ceiling painting in the Blue Drawing Room may show Peace banishing War from the Four Continents

speculating on the French stock market, and by May 1720 had accumulated a paper fortune of 6.5 million livres. But then John Law's Mississippi Company collapsed, and the Marquess, a vacillating figure who was always under his daughter's thumb, found himself facing debts of £170,000. Bailiffs moved into Powis House, and writs flew between members of the family. In 1722 the Marquess was restored to his ancient titles and estates, but he was obliged to remain in France and serve time in a Paris gaol to avoid his creditors. The castle was also seriously damaged by fire in the 1720s. Once again, the family was rescued by the lead mine, where production tripled between 1725 and 1729. Despite having got her fingers so badly burnt, Lady Mary continued to speculate on Spanish gold and mines in the New World – with equal lack of success. But by the 1740s, income from the lead mine was declining, and the Marquess was in no position to bail her out once more.

WILLIAM, 3RD MARQUESS OF POWIS
(*c.*1698–1748)

The 3rd Marquess was almost 50 when he succeeded in 1745, but although deep in debt, he seems never to have considered finding himself a rich wife. He died only three years later still unmarried, and according to one witness, he 'never went to bed sober in the last ten years of his life'.

(Left) The Marquess Gate

(Right) The 2nd Marquess commissioned Gerard Lanscroon to paint the murals on the Grand Staircase

NEW MONEY AND NEW DEBTS

HENRY ARTHUR, 1ST EARL OF POWIS
(1703–72)

The last Marquess's obvious heir was his niece, Barbara Herbert, the last Catholic member of the family, but by this stage, thanks to Lady Mary's disastrous speculations, few of the family were on speaking terms. So, instead, he left Powis to his ninth cousin, Henry Arthur Herbert of Chirbury, reckoning that, as a successful Shropshire land-owner, he would have the wherewithal to revive the estate. He also recognised that Henry was a loyal Protestant, who had raised a regiment to oppose the Jacobite rising of Bonnie Prince Charlie in 1745, and so was better able to persuade George II to revive the Powis peerage, which would otherwise have died out with him. The calculation proved correct: three months after Henry inherited, he became the 1st Earl of Powis of the second creation. However, there were dark rumours that the last Marquess had been drunk when he made his will, and Barbara Herbert's guardian, Lord Montague, threatened to challenge it. The solution was simple: in 1751 Henry married Barbara. He was 48, she was only 16, and described as 'a very good-humoured, inoffensive girle'. She inherited the family addic-tion to gambling (Horace Walpole called her 'a macaroni rake'), but despite this, their marriage was happy, if occasionally stormy. The 1st Earl also had his reckless side, having spent more than £20,000 to get himself elected as MP for Ludlow between 1727 and 1743. To try and settle their debts, Powis had to be placed in the hands of trustees, and their estates at Hendon and in Northamptonshire sold. But the 1st Earl calculated that he still owed £306,175 8s 4d.

In 1771 he was obliged to sell his old family home at Oakly Park in Shropshire to Clive of India (beginning what was to be a significant association), and move permanently to Powis. In preparation for

(Left, top) Henry Arthur, 1st Earl of Powis; attributed to Thomas Hudson (no. 47; Long Gallery)

(Left) George, 2nd Earl of Powis; painted by Pompeo Batoni in Rome in 1776 (no. 63; Oak Drawing Room)

The north front in the 1790s

moving in, he commissioned a survey of the castle from the Shropshire architect Thomas Farnolls Pritchard. The conclusions were alarming: Pritchard found the terrace balustrades in 'a ruinous condition' and the roof leads 'in very indifferent repair'. But he appreciated the historical importance of Edward Herbert's Elizabethan apartment and the 17th-century State Bedroom: 'This whole appartment has a most Elegant appearance, and shou'd be preserved to keep up the Stile and Dignity of the Old Castle'. He also proposed changes, but before these could be implemented, the 1st Earl died, in 1772.

GEORGE, 2ND EARL OF POWIS
(1755–1801)

The 2nd Earl succeeded at the age of seventeen, and three years later set out on a Grand Tour of Italy in the company of the Scottish painter William Patoun. In Rome in 1776 he was painted by the most fashionable portraitist of the day, Pompeo Batoni. He also took classes with the dealer-antiquarian James Byres, who may have encouraged him to buy the *pietra dura* table in the Long Gallery.

On his return in 1776, the 2nd Earl celebrated his coming-of-age in Pritchard's newly completed Ballroom; Pritchard's other proposals were rejected as too expensive. In any case, the 2nd Earl seems to have preferred life in the capital, where he could indulge 'the prodigalities of London and driving high phaetons up St James Street', according to Lord Torrington, who visited Powis in 1784:

It is grievous to see the devastation that long neglect and late winds have committed on this place; as some great windows are quite forc'd in, and the hangings are waving in the air! There is a long gallery fill'd with family pictures; and some pompous bed chambers, but all in dampness, & uninhabited.

On his death in 1801 the 2nd Earl left debts of £177,000, but no son.

THE 19TH CENTURY

EDWARD, 2ND EARL OF POWIS
(3rd creation) (1785–1848)

The Powis estates passed to Edward Clive, the son of the 2nd Earl's sister Henrietta, who had married Edward, Lord Clive, the son of the conqueror of India (see family tree on inside back cover). But in 1801 the younger Edward Clive was only sixteen, and so his father managed the estate on his behalf until he came of age. The elder Edward Clive also brought to Powis perhaps its greatest treasure – the famous collection of Indian artefacts assembled by his father, his wife and himself. As Governor of Madras, he had fought in the war against Tipu Sahib, Sultan of Mysore. On 4 May 1799 British troops killed Tipu Sahib and captured his capital at Seringapatam. In the process Lord Clive acquired numerous relics of Tipu, including the magnificent state tent of painted chintz and the jewelled tiger's head. These are now displayed in the Clive Museum. In recognition of his service in India and of his son's inheritance of Powis, the Powis earldom was recreated for him in 1804.

When the younger Edward Clive reached 21, he inherited Powis, and as the terms of the will decreed, changed his surname from Clive to Herbert (during his father's lifetime, he bore the courtesy title Viscount Clive). He came into an estate which had been transformed by his father's careful management. The debts had been settled by selling outlying land, and although the acreage shrank, annual income rose between 1801 and 1845 from £14,000 to £24,000. He was now in a position to modernise the castle, to which little had been done for a hundred years. Clive was a Tory and he turned to the favourite architect of the Tory establishment, Sir Robert Smirke, who mended the roof and remodelled some of the less

(Right, top) Edward, 1st Earl of Powis managed the estates until his son, who had inherited them, came of age; pastel by H. D. Hamilton (no. 102; Blue Drawing Room)

(Right) Henrietta Herbert, the last of the Herberts of Powis, who married the 1st Earl in 1784; by Sir Joshua Reynolds (no. 2; Dining Room)

historic interiors in a vaguely Adam style in 1815–18. The Library was recast to receive Viscount Clive's important collection of rare books, which included many early manuscripts and volumes from the Empress Josephine's library at Malmaison. (Many of these were sold at Sotheby's in 1923.) His marriage in 1818 to Lady Lucy Graham was celebrated with barrels of beer in the park, while the garden fountains ran with wine. In August 1832 the couple welcomed the thirteen-year-old Princess Victoria, who admired 'the little old windows jutting in and out and a fine gallery with a dry-rubbed floor and some beautiful busts'. In 1847 the 2nd Earl was narrowly defeated by Victoria's consort, Prince Albert, for the Chancellorship of Cambridge University.

During a pheasant shoot in January 1848, Lord Powis was accidently hit in the leg by one of his sons (who thereafter bore the cruel nickname of 'Bag-Dad'). He was carried back to the castle, but died ten days later.

EDWARD, 3RD EARL OF POWIS
(1818–91)

The 3rd Earl's coming-of-age in 1839 was celebrated with a ball in the castle, tea and buns for a thousand in a marquee in the park, and the foundation of a new church in Welshpool:

A goodly presage thus displayed
Of pious resolutions –
That Church and State in Powisland
May always hold together.

The 3rd Earl was a scholar and a bachelor. In his youth he had been a member of Disraeli's 'Young England' movement, and he served as MP for North Shropshire for five years and as Lord Lieutenant of Montgomeryshire from 1877 until his death. But he was not interested in a wider public career, and when Disraeli offered to appoint him Viceroy of India in 1875, he simply scribbled on the outside of the envelope, 'Not worth considering – Powis'. He made few changes to the castle.

(Left, top) Edward, 2nd Earl of Powis; by Sir Francis Grant (no. 70; Ballroom)

(Left) Edward, 3rd Earl of Powis

THE 20TH CENTURY

The 3rd Earl's nephew, George, inherited at the age of 30 in 1891, having married Violet Lane-Fox the previous year. She concentrated on reviving the garden; he brought the castle into the modern era.

Puzzled why smoke should be appearing at the foot of the Grand Staircase, the 4th Earl had the floorboards taken up. He was alarmed to discover the cause: the central heating pipes were getting so hot that they were actually charring the floor joists. He also wanted to get rid of Smirke's early 19th-century changes, which he thought 'incongruous and not in keeping with the Castle'. On entering one particularly cheerless bedroom, a guest had complimented Lady Powis on her clever conversion of the dungeons. He turned to the architect G. F. Bodley, having been impressed by the sensitive restoration work he had done on another fragile 17th-century building, Ham House in Surrey. Bodley was commissioned to remodel the Dining Room, the Oak Drawing Room and several other major interiors in the spirit of Sir

Violet, Countess of Powis, who revived the garden; by Ellis Roberts (no. 14; Dining Room)

George, 4th Earl of Powis, who bequeathed Powis to the Trust; by Sir William Llewellyn (no. 17; Dining Room)

Edward Herbert's Elizabethan Long Gallery. Bodley provided not only new heraldic chimney-pieces and plasterwork friezes, but also boldly patterned curtains, furnishing fabrics from Watts & Co., and intricately decorated door handles.

The 4th Earl suffered a series of family tragedies. His elder son, Percy, died of his wounds while serving as a captain in the Welsh Guards at the Battle of the Somme in September 1916. His wife died after a car crash in 1929, and his only surviving son, Mervyn, was killed in a plane crash while on active service in 1942. At the time, Powis was being occupied by the Welsh Girls School, which had been evacuated from Ashford in Middlesex.

On his death in 1952 he bequeathed Powis Castle with an endowment to the National Trust, but his uncle's great-grandson, the 8th and present Earl of Powis, retains an apartment in the castle.